THE DISCIPLINE POCI

By Stuart Emmett

Drawings by Phil Hailstone

"Covers an area of people management that many are afraid to venture into – a straightforward and informative but light-hearted approach for any manager or student."
Donald Butcher, DAB Consultants

Published by:
Management Pocketbooks Ltd
14 East Street, Alresford, Hants SO24 9EE, U.K.
Tel: +44 (0)1962 735573   Fax: +44 (0)1962 733637
E-mail: sales@pocketbook.co.uk
Website: www.pocketbook.co.uk

This edition published 2001

© Stuart Emmett 2001

ISBN 1 870471 90 3

Design, Typeset & Graphics by **artsFX Ltd**   Printed in U.K.

Note: The author has made best endeavours not to include anything that, if used, would be injurious or cause financial loss to the user. The user is, however, strongly recommended before applying or using any of the contents, to check and verify their own company policy/requirements. No liability will therefore be accepted by the author for the use of any of the contents.

CONTENTS

UNDERSTANDING
DISCIPLINE & GRIEVANCE

FOCUS ON BEHAVIOUR

First, you need to appreciate that discipline involves handling the behaviour of apparently 'problem people'.

'Problem people' key facts:

- The behaviour is the problem, **not** the person
- Seeing people as a problem can be dangerous and destructive, in relationships and in managing people
- It is vital to separate out the person from the problem

A 'problem person' is someone whose behaviour does not meet the normal standard we expect. It follows, therefore, that we will need to be clear what the standard expected is. We will look at this shortly.

DEFINING DISCIPLINE

Dictionary definitions of discipline mention:

- Instruction
- Maintaining order
- Mental training
- A system of rules
- Controlling behaviour

IS DISCIPLINE PUNISHMENT?

The view of discipline as punishment
may originate from childhood associations,
and the view that discipline is all about
a 'wrong' to be 'corrected'.

A balance needs to be struck
between viewing discipline as
punishment or improvement.

THE IMPROVEMENT/PUNISHMENT BALANCE

To punish is to:

- Cause the offender to suffer
- Inflict a penalty
- Chastise
- Give a penalty for wrongdoing
- Reprimand
- Correct

To improve is to:

- Make better
- Use for good purpose
- Become better
- Progress
- Be more prosperous

THE IMPROVEMENT/PUNISHMENT BALANCE

Conclusion:

The key aim of discipline at work is to encourage unsatisfactory employees to improve.
(The word discipline derives from the Latin verb *discere*. This means to teach or mould.)

Keeping the focus on improvement means having a view that discipline is about trying to gain, and not using blame.

BLAME OR GAIN VIEWPOINTS

Perception is reality - so how we see things is important. Consider the following lists:

List A

I am right, I know best

Listen to me

Seeing obstacles and problems

Finding fault

List B

I would like to know your opinion

Let me listen to your view

Seeing solutions and opportunities

Giving support

UNDERSTANDING DISCIPLINE & GRIEVANCE

BLAME OR GAIN VIEWPOINTS

List A

Feeling frustrated when with people

Making others feel guilty

Looking for **who** is wrong

Mistakes are to be punished

List B

Feeling calm when with people

Making people learn

Looking for **what** is wrong

Mistakes are opportunities to learn

List A is all about blame, List B is more about gain.

As perception is reality, then seeing discipline as punishment will involve you taking more of a blame view! This will not help, but will have an effect upon, and be shown in, your handling of discipline issues.

WHEN IS PUNISHMENT VALID?

You should use punishment as a final sanction only, when everything else has failed.

Remember, the prime objectives have to relate to gaining an improvement.

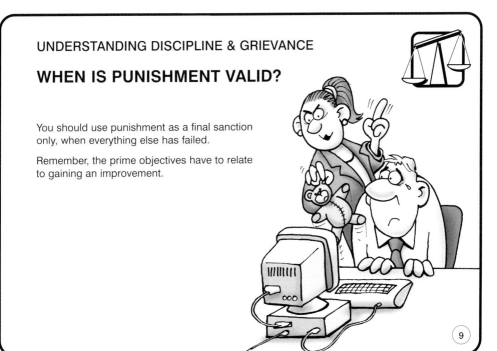

UNDERSTANDING DISCIPLINE & GRIEVANCE

KEY FACTS

Discipline is:

- Conforming to a system of rules for conduct
- Ways and norms and expectations of behaviour
- Sometimes *hidden* in people's/companies' beliefs and values
- Usually accepted as necessary by the majority
- Sometimes imposed by mandatory legislation
- Visible when relationships between a company and an employee are unsatisfactory to the company
- One of the measures that helps employees keep to the standards expected
- A way to help employees improve
- A way companies can deal fairly with those who do not keep to the standards

PRIME OBJECTIVES

The prime objectives for disciplining need to be concerned with:

- Improving, correcting, preventing, re-aligning

- Bringing about conformity to standards

- Encouraging improvement, and higher levels of performance

MISCONDUCT OFFENCES

Offences can always be categorised as either performance issues or relationship/behavioural issues.

Work **performance** issues are about:
- Poor attendance and absence
- Poor/careless work output
- Failure to follow rules, such as health and safety

Work **relationship** issues are about:
- Refusal to obey reasonable instructions
- Disruptive behaviour

Note: Misconduct offences normally lead to disciplinary action, whereas the following gross misconduct offences normally lead to dismissal.

GROSS MISCONDUCT OFFENCES

Again, these offences can be categorised as either performance or relationship issues.

Work **performance** issues are:
- Gross negligence causing loss, damage
- Serious disregard of health and safety legislation
- Deliberate damage to company property

Work **relationship** issues are:
- Theft, fraud
- Assault, fighting
- Conduct prejudicial to the company's reputation
- Serious incapability due to alcohol, illegal drugs
- Gross insubordination

Note: Misconduct offences (see previous page) normally lead to disciplinary action, but gross misconduct normally leads to dismissal.

DEFINING GRIEVANCE

Dictionary definitions of grievance are:

- Grounds for complaint
- A cause of grief
- Uneasiness
- Distress

A grievance might originate from any one of a number of sources. As a manager, you need to be able to listen actively to grievances. It will help if you appreciate the following key facts.

KEY FACTS ABOUT GRIEVANCES

Grievances are often below the surface - they are the moans and groans that provide fodder for the grapevine. They are the hygiene factors of the Herzberg view of motivation: those issues that need to be *cleaned up* to maintain a sense of order. They include such items as:

- Working conditions
- Supervision
- Interpersonal relationships
- Company policies and how they are administered
- Money
- Job security
- Status

KEY FACTS ABOUT GRIEVANCES

Grievances surface and become visible when the relationship between a company and the employee is unsatisfactory to the employee, and the employee is prepared to bring this, formally, to the management's attention.

This is the formal side - clearly, grievances bubble below the surface before the formal process takes over. Good management is able to deal satisfactorily with grievances before they become formalised.

PRIME OBJECTIVES

The prime objectives for handling grievances need to be concerned with:

- Providing a means for employees to offload, unburden and release themselves

- Having a consistent and equal procedure to resolve disagreements

TYPICAL GRIEVANCES

Grievances can be about anything at all. Some examples follow, covering relationship and company issues:

Work relationship issues:

I am treated badly by x
I cannot get on with y
I am made to feel small
I am not appreciated by the company

Company issues:

On policy	-	*We were told to work on a Saturday and we never do that*
On administration	-	*It takes three months for expenses to be paid*
On work conditions	-	*This place is too cold and too dirty*
On wages	-	*X is paid more than me and we do the same job*
About the canteen	-	*The food is poor, and expensive*

STAYING POSITIVE

1. An understandable reaction from many managers who have to deal with discipline and grievance procedures is, 'I do not want to hurt their feelings', or 'I do not want another argument'.

2. This indicates a negative approach. Having a positive view leads you to see discipline as a way of encouraging people to succeed, and as something that provides guidance and direction, for both manager and employees.

3. A positive view of grievances can lead to remedial action that prevents later disciplinary problems (which often arise out of frustration).

4. Always remember that a problem is a deviation from something expected.

5. Remember also that improvement is the better side of the improvement/punishment balance.

HANDLING
TYPICAL PROBLEMS

ROOT CAUSES

The root causes of discipline problems are:
- 70% frustration
- 20% gain (eg: stealing time, theft)
- 10% all the other reasons

When frustrations are left to *fester*, they can build up and become the cause behind many discipline and grievance issues. Spending time on prevention can be better than having to spend time on the cure. (See pages 73 and following.)

Meanwhile, we have seen that misconduct is found in two areas:

- Unacceptable performance
- Unacceptable relationships

UNACCEPTABLE PERFORMANCE

Definition: Work performance that is not up to the standard expected.

It is important to use this definition, as then any misconduct under discussion is clearly going to relate to standards that were expected, but have not been met.

Being clear on the standards expected is therefore essential.

UNACCEPTABLE PERFORMANCE

SMART OBJECTIVES & STANDARDS

Using SMART objectives will give a clear view when performance is below the standard expected.

SMART means setting objectives/standards that are **S**imple, **M**easurable, **A**ttainable, **R**ealistic, and **T**ime based.

Determining SMART objectives and standards:

- Objectives are about the job and identify key outcomes
- Standards and targets are measurable outcomes using measures of quality, quantity, time and cost
- Standards are achievable by all, they are the norm and are common to all
- Targets are individually agreed with those who can exceed the standard

UNACCEPTABLE PERFORMANCE

CANNOT OR WILL NOT

When performance is not met, then there is a need to establish if the person:

- **Cannot do it,** or
- **Will not do it**

The former is usually clear and noticeable. However, the latter may be camouflaged and not easily seen. The underpinning reasons for the non-performance will have to be investigated.

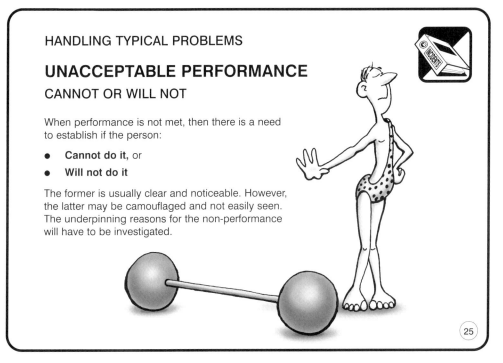

UNACCEPTABLE PERFORMANCE

FINDING THE REASONS

- **What reasons are there when someone cannot do their work as required?**
There are many possible reasons, one of which might be insufficient training. Common factors, however, will be lack of **competence** and not having the necessary knowledge/skills to do the job.

- **What reasons are there when someone will not do their work as required?**
There are many possible reasons, one of which might be dissatisfaction over something. But the common factors will be a lack of personal **commitment** through not having the confidence and/or the motivation/desire to do the job as required.

Solving each of these requires a different approach.

UNACCEPTABLE PERFORMANCE

COMPETENCE & COMMITMENT

Solving competence issues:

- Give the required training/tools/resources to do the job
- If they still cannot do it, check for understanding
- If they still cannot do it, maybe they are not up to it, therefore consider arranging a transfer to another, simpler job

Solving commitment issues:

- The key to this is raising morale and motivation, which we look at in greater detail in a later section: Spend Time on Prevention

UNACCEPTABLE PERFORMANCE

WHEN TO DISCIPLINE

Before considering disciplining over a performance issue, ensure that:

- **SMART** objectives, standards, targets are used and are understood
- It is not a competence issue
- It is not a commitment issue

If you have satisfied yourself on all of the above:

- Investigate fully
- Review with a colleague before deciding what to do

UNACCEPTABLE ATTENDANCE/ UNAUTHORISED ABSENCE

At its extreme, this type of misconduct offence is about stealing time from employers.

Absence rates of over 5% should give cause for concern; anything over 10% is serious. The problems caused by absence are as follows:

- Colleagues have to cover for absentees, creating extra work, and leading to stress and poor morale
- The company incurs extra costs, for example in overtime rates or temporary staff
- The customer (potentially) experiences poor quality work, late deliveries, unexpected delays

HANDLING TYPICAL PROBLEMS

UNACCEPTABLE ATTENDANCE/ UNAUTHORISED ABSENCE

Suggestions for dealing with absence problems are:

- Start by considering the morale and motivation at work, as absence is often a good indicator of the motivation *temperature*.

- Follow the company policy

- Be consistent in your approach

- Establish the facts, investigate

- Explore the problem - for example, if the absence is due to illness/injury, then make medical support and advice available

- Consider any special circumstances

- Look for the reasons underpinning the absence

- Review the possible actions with others

- Establish the best course of action to take

UNACCEPTABLE RELATIONSHIPS/BEHAVIOUR

When dealing with relationship offences, first check out possible causes for the unacceptable behaviour.

- Some **external** causes may be cultural differences, lack of resources or changing society norms. These may not always be discipline offences but instead may require a manager to show greater flexibility and tolerance. For example:
  - we live in a multi-cultural society and need to understand others' values/beliefs
  - we cannot always give all the required resources
  - we live in a society that is changing rapidly

UNACCEPTABLE RELATIONSHIPS/BEHAVIOUR

- Some **internal** causes of unacceptable behaviour may be a person's personality, skills, or level of maturity. These may not give rise to discipline offences but, again, require flexibility and tolerance from a manager.

  For example:
  - different mixes of people can be valuable
  - selection testing/specific training may be needed
  - the *world view* held by a person will vary depending on exposure, self motivation and self awareness

CHOOSING THE RIGHT APPROACH

When should I counsel, coach or discipline?

Counselling is an early step in solving work-based problems about performance and relationships:

- It is a supportive discussion, involving sympathetic listening
- It is **not** a directive discussion with heavy *telling*

Guidelines for carrying out counselling follow.

Coaching may then be a subsequent step where managers work closely with an employee to see and support them through work-related problems.

Remember that discipline is the last step to resolve work-related problems about performance and relationships. It is to be applied only when everything else has failed.

GUIDELINES FOR COUNSELLING

- Before conducting counselling yourself, you need to decide if a more experienced counsellor is required

- Remember, the role of counselling is to solve the employee's problem by giving insight

- Counselling is used to help the employee develop a plan to solve their problem

- If you cannot be supportive to those who may be angry or anxious, then you should not counsel. Find someone else to do it

GUIDELINES FOR COUNSELLING

How to do it:

- Get the employee to talk
- Be understanding and show empathy
- Listen actively
- Provide the opportunity to talk at length; this can sometimes itself be the solution
- Keep the focus on performance and **not** on personality - you want an improvement in performance, you cannot change their personality
- The atmosphere should be one of mutual respect

Follow the three-step rule for counselling:

1. Explore with open and general questions
2. Help the employee to see their problem
3. Support the employee as they move towards a solution

THREE-STEP MODEL

When investigating problem behaviour, having a clear structure to use will help to ensure consistency and uniformity of approach. Use the three-step model to determine whether the formal disciplinary procedure is the right way to proceed.

The Three-Step Model:
(Getting it right - first time - every time)

Step 3 - Establish what action is needed — **DECIDE 3**

Step 2 - Explore the problem — **CHECK 2**

Step 1 - Establish the facts — **INVESTIGATE 1**

THREE-STEP MODEL

 Step 1: Establish the facts (investigate)

- A problem person is one whose performance or behaviour is not meeting the normal standard expected

- Performance and behaviour are, essentially, what people do and/or say

- You are trying to shape and redefine performance and behaviour to the expected standard

You need to be very clear when recording performance and behaviour that you use objective facts and not subjective feelings.

The latter includes personal opinions and emotions, which may distort the facts. The former attempts to be more objective.

Keeping an incidents diary will help you to keep an objective record, see page 47.

HANDLING TYPICAL PROBLEMS

THREE-STEP MODEL

 Step 1: Establish the facts (investigate)

Record the facts by using the questioning approach. Ask:

- What happened?
- When did it happen?
- Where did it happen?
- Why did it happen?
- How did it happen?
- Who was involved?

This approach establishes objective facts, which need to be emotion free, and show how things went wrong. For example, if you say to someone 'You were late' it is subjective; saying 'Three of us saw you arrive at 0915 hours; you were 15 minutes late' is objective.

To establish facts successfully involves personal observation. This is recorded by a signed statement, which must focus on the facts.

THREE-STEP MODEL

 Step 2: Explore the problem (check)

Having established the facts in Step 1, you need to explore the problem further by:

- Looking to see if there is anything significant about the deviation from *where they should be* to *where they actually are*. You are looking at the deviation from the standard expected.

- Looking to see what type of offence it may be; for example, misconduct or gross misconduct?

- Looking to see what type of issue it may be; for example, performance or relationship/behavioural?

HANDLING TYPICAL PROBLEMS

THREE-STEP MODEL

 Step 2: Explore the problem (check)

Examples of deviations from standards and *expectations* in rules and procedures can be:

- Timekeeping   - eg: clocking in late
- Absence   - eg: unauthorised absence
- Health and safety   - eg: not following the *duty of care*
- Discrimination   - eg: verbally abusing others
- Use of company facilities - eg: private phone call

Deviations from standards and *expectations* could result from significant and one-off special events such as:

- Personal circumstances - eg: *domestics*
- Work relationships   - eg: personality clashes
- Job factors   - eg: boredom
- Work conditions   - eg: physical noise

THREE-STEP MODEL

Step 2: Explore the problem (check)

From a formal discipline and grievance point of view, these deviations from standards and *expectations* can be categorised as follows:

- Grievances are dissatisfaction/disagreement/complaints about work conditions, work relationships, or job factors

- Disciplines are:
  - Misconduct offences such as poor timekeeping, unreasonable absence, failure to follow health and safety rules, and any behaviour that disrupts working relationships
  - Gross misconduct offences such as theft, fraud, fighting, gross negligence, serious disregard for health and safety, serious incapability, gross insubordination, and unauthorised entry to company records

THREE-STEP MODEL

 Step 3: Establish the action needed (decide)

You have now established the facts and have explored the problem. The next stage is to investigate and check before taking a decision about what action is needed.

The possible actions are as follows:

- Do nothing
- Get the circumstance/situation changed
- Get the person to change

We will now look at each of these.

THREE-STEP MODEL

 Step 3: Establish the action needed (decide)

If you do **nothing** then it is highly likely that the problem will:

- Grow and deteriorate
- Show the manager is a procrastinator who never takes decisive action
- Lower the morale of others

The only time the *do nothing* option is valid is when there has been found to be no problem.

43

THREE-STEP MODEL

 Step 3: Establish the action needed (decide)

If you decide to **change the circumstances**, then this is valid when:

- You have looked at the *before* (those triggers of behaviour) which has caused the *after* (those deviations from the standard). These are the consequences of the behaviour

- You have investigated the observable *after*

- You have determined which *before* cause needs changing to give a different effect

- You are satisfied it is possible to make the change

THREE-STEP MODEL

Step 3: Establish the action needed (decide)

Your third option is to get the person to change. How can you do this?

At a deeper psychological level, you cannot be expected to be involved. At a more superficial level of changing attitudes, then you are able to look at the following:

- Counselling, talking and listening, listening, listening
- Coaching and training
- Using the discipline procedures

THREE-STEP MODEL

 Step 3: Establish the action needed (decide)

Finally, remember that using the discipline procedures can have serious consequences, so it is essential to review:

- Step back and look again.
- Has this happened before?
- When?
- How was it tackled before?
- Who are you dealing with?
- Do you need to approach more people?
- What do others suggest?
- What does company policy say?
- What does your boss think?
- What do your HR/Personnel people think?

After the final review, make your decision and write it up in your incidents diary.

KEEPING AN INCIDENTS DIARY

- Documentation is important in handling discipline and grievance procedures. Good documentation is an important part of these procedures.

- Keeping an incidents diary will help you to explain what happened.

- It is an on-going record of a manager's efforts to help others succeed.

MON 21 JULY
9.30 Meeting with Ralph about his conduct....

11.30 Give good performance award to Jackie Smith

2.00 Sort out training course for Alan Brown

4.00 Lunch with team leader. .....

KEEPING AN INCIDENTS DIARY

Things to record in the diary or log are as follows:

- Conversations about job performance
- Informal counselling
- Disciplinary action
- Good performance
- Explanations
- Training undertaken

Keeping such a diary will save you time and effort in the end. It will help to demonstrate your objectivity and to show that you have followed the rules and procedures.

THE NEED FOR
RULES & PROCEDURES

THE NEED FOR RULES & PROCEDURES

LEGAL ASPECTS

If you employ over 20 people then, by law, written details are required of the discipline and grievance rules and procedures.

Whilst you may slightly vary the procedures, it is the main aspects to be covered that are dealt with in this publication. These main aspects cannot be made *tougher*, but may be *relaxed*.

Recommended reading is the Code of Practice from the UK Government Advisory Conciliation and Arbitration Service (ACAS). Their website address is acas.org.uk.

THE NEED FOR RULES & PROCEDURES

RULES

You need rules:

- To set standards of conduct

- To show the way people should behave

- To clarify what is expected

GUIDELINES FOR RULES

- Keep them simple, clear and easy to understand
- Put them in writing
- Display them publicly
- Keep them up to date
- Explain what type of offences (minor misconduct, serious misconduct, gross misconduct) will be dealt with by the discipline procedures
- Explain what issues can be dealt with by the grievance procedures

PROCEDURES

You need procedures:

- To help people keep to the rules
- To establish the methods used to deal with the rules
- To maintain and apply the standards
- To demonstrate a fair and consistent approach
- To bring clarity

SAMPLE DISCIPLINE PROCEDURES (DP)

STAGE	OFFENCE	POSSIBLE OUTCOME	REMAINS ON RECORD
One	Minor	Verbal warning	Six months
Two	Minor repeated, or first serious	First written warning	One year

THE NEED FOR RULES & PROCEDURES

SAMPLE DISCIPLINE PROCEDURES (DP)

STAGE	OFFENCE	POSSIBLE OUTCOME	REMAINS ON RECORD
Three	Repeated, or gross misconduct	Final written warning or suspension or dismissal	Two years
Four	Repeated, or after investigation	Dismissal	–

Note: Before the DP, investigations and fact gathering are needed. After the DP, appeals and formal reviews are needed.

The progressive nature of the procedures allows for fairness and for recovery of situations.

THE NEED FOR RULES & PROCEDURES

SAMPLE GRIEVANCE PROCEDURES (GP)

STAGE	INTERVIEW	OUTCOME
One	Informal discussion	Resolved or not
Two	Formal discussion: employee/supervisor	Resolved or not

THE NEED FOR RULES & PROCEDURES

SAMPLE GRIEVANCE PROCEDURES (GP)

STAGE	INTERVIEW	OUTCOME
Three	Formal discussion: employee/next level up	Resolved or not
Four	Formal discussion: employee/next level up, final decision	Resolved, but if not then the employee may choose to leave

Note: In formal discussions it is required that all details are in writing, and that minutes and notes of meeting are kept.

The progressive nature of the procedures allows for fairness and for solutions.

THE NEED FOR RULES & PROCEDURES

PROCEDURES CHECKLIST

It is important you know, in detail, your company procedures.
Are you able to say *yes* to all of the following?

1. Do you know your company's formal procedures?

2. Do you require investigations before starting the procedures?

3. Do different people from the ones who are involved in the formal interviewing undertake investigations?

4. Are employees free to choose who will help/represent them in the formal procedures/interviews?

5. Are employees required to notify the employer in advance of any representative/witness they wish to attend the formal procedures/interview?

PROCEDURES CHECKLIST

6. Is the employer required to notify the employee of those who will be present at the interview?

7. Does the employer require more than one manager to be present at the interview?

8. Does the employer specify procedures for the interviews?

9. Does the employer say how a record of the interviews will be made/kept?

You must be confident that you know the answers to all these questions.

If in doubt, check it out.

THE NEED FOR RULES & PROCEDURES

LEGAL ASPECTS REVISITED

Legal case law says that:

- Employee investigations must be *adequate*

- Employees must be told that *discipline* is taking place in accordance with the company discipline procedures

- Employees must be told in advance what the *charge* is

- Employees must be given sufficient notice of all interviews

- Employees must be given adequate opportunity to provide an explanation

- Employees must be given opportunity to be accompanied by a helper/representative

- Employees being dismissed must be given the opportunity of an appeal to a senior manager

THE NEED FOR RULES & PROCEDURES

FAIRNESS & CONSISTENCY

What happens if we do not have fair and consistent procedures?

- People get away with poor work performance
- Management authority is undermined
- Employees become demoralised
- It becomes difficult to take any corrective action

FAIRNESS & CONSISTENCY

- Legal requirements need an *adequate* investigation to show a **sincere** effort is made to resolve problems for all people
- The progressive nature of procedures shows that a **reasonable** effort is made to resolve problems for all people
- Consistency will stop different applications by different managers on the same site or discrepancies between different sites in the same company
- Consistency ensures managers follow 'the book' to prevent subsequent changes of mind, loss of credibility, time, and cost

COMMUNICATING THE PROCEDURES

It is a requirement that everyone in the company knows the procedures.

Communication is all about the following:

- An exchange of information, a two way process, to ensure understanding
- The objective of communication is to stop misunderstanding

Communication is often badly undertaken, because:

- It is not two way
- Understanding is not tested

Remember, the **meaning of communication is in its effect**, so be sure the effect is about understanding.

THE NEED FOR RULES & PROCEDURES

MEANS & METHODS OF COMMUNICATION

- ❏ Written   - eg: memos, reports
- ❏ Verbal   - eg: one to ones, meetings
- ❏ Visual   - eg: pictures, diagrams
- ❏ Hearing   - eg: words
- ❏ Feeling   - eg: tone of voice

Methods of Communication

- ❏ Direct   - eg: face to face (the responses are immediate and can be seen, heard and felt)
- ❏ Indirect   - eg: telephone, memos, e-mails (the responses are delayed)
- ❏ Reading   - eg: rule books, job descriptions
- ❏ Showing   - eg: giving examples
- ❏ Doing   - eg: role playing with feedback

Whatever the means or method of communication, it should be **KISS** (**K**eep **I**t **S**hort and **S**imple) and it should be understood.

64

THE NEED FOR RULES & PROCEDURES

TIMING OF COMMUNICATION

Procedures can be communicated to employees at the following times:

- ❏ During recruitment
- ❏ During inductions
- ❏ In job descriptions
- ❏ In appraisals

What should be covered?

- ❏ General standards of conduct
- ❏ Specific standards for a job

CONTRACT OF EMPLOYMENT

THE NEED FOR RULES & PROCEDURES

DURING RECRUITMENT

Procedures can be communicated during the recruitment process

- Be clear in the job specification
- Restate and tell the person:
  - the general standards, eg: the hours of attendance and what to do if there is a problem
  - the specific standards, eg: the number of orders you expect an order clerk to process per shift
- Ask if they understand
- Test their understanding; do not assume that because you have said it they have understood

THE NEED FOR RULES & PROCEDURES

DURING INDUCTION

Procedures can be communicated during induction

- Advise what the requirements are, eg: as a minimum, the following:
  - rules, eg: attendance, sickness, holidays
  - health and safety; eg: accidents, need for protective clothing
  - security, eg: pass systems, search procedures
- Give out the terms and conditions on Disciplines and Grievances (description of procedures, types of offences)
- Set the *ground rules* for job specifics and general issues
- Record what has been done

It is a good idea to spread the induction process over a couple of weeks to avoid overload.

THE NEED FOR RULES & PROCEDURES

IN JOB DESCRIPTIONS

Procedures can be communicated in job descriptions

- Discuss job description with the employee
- Ask questions to ensure and test understanding
- Clarify responses
- Record what has been done

THE NEED FOR RULES & PROCEDURES

IN APPRAISALS

Procedures can be communicated in appraisals

- Say how the employee is doing
- Review the job description for validity
- Offer any guidance needed
- State your aspirations, as their manager
- Have an open and frank discussion
- Restate and review any discipline issues

THE NEED FOR RULES & PROCEDURES

MANAGEMENT FUNCTIONS

How do procedures fit with the management functions?

- Planning function
    - in determining the outcomes needed, in establishing policies, in developing procedures

- Organising function
    - in defining authority levels, in structuring work relationships

- Directing/Co-ordinating function
    - in communicating, in determining the level of effectiveness

- Controlling function
    - in using standards, in creating measures, in taking corrective action, in making improvements

Rules and procedures are therefore fundamental to efficient and effective management.

MONITOR & REVIEW

It is essential to monitor and review all procedures

- Recognise that procedures do change and that legislation can be amended.

- For example, in 1999 and 2000 changes were made to reduce the two-year qualifying rule to one year and to representation being a legal right for workers and employees. More legislation is expected on human rights generally.

- New policy and communication will be needed to cover the changes.

SPEND TIME ON PREVENTION

PREVENTION IS BETTER THAN CURE

We said earlier that spending time on preventing problems and misconduct could be worthwhile. There is also the viewpoint that a problem is an opportunity in disguise!

Consider the following:

- Employee's question: *Have you got a minute?*
  Manager's answer: *No, I am busy. Go and see personnel; it is nothing to do with me.*
  The employee then gets frustrated.

- An employee misunderstands a simple issue and, when trying to find out more, can find no one to listen or show interest. This leads to resentment; the issue grows into a problem, leading in turn to grievance, dissatisfaction, depression, frustration, poor work, and finally the discipline procedure.

Damage has been caused here when an opportunity was actually available to prevent future problems.

SPEND TIME ON PREVENTION

MORALE & MOTIVATION AT WORK

The general atmosphere at work affects people and how they behave. So, this atmosphere will affect the discipline and grievance issues you have to deal with.

Poor morale at work will exist where:

- Management shows no interest in employees
- Objectives are not understood
- Employees are given no feedback
- Employees feel they cannot influence management
- Favouritism is shown
- Rules are not fairly and equally applied
- There is little job satisfaction

- Managers do not know their people
- There is only destructive criticism
- There is little *team spirit*
- Poor performance is not dealt with
- Poor relationships are not dealt with
- Unacceptable behaviour is not dealt with
- Unacceptable absence is not dealt with

RAISING MORALE

Morale at work is raised by:

- Ensuring the opposite of the factors (previous page) that bring about poor morale
- Good and effective leadership
- Management styles more supportive than directive
- Self discipline
- Good communication
- Employees' involvement in decisions
- Managers who know that management is not just about technical, objective, hard skills, but also involves subjective emotions and applying soft skills

SPEND TIME ON PREVENTION

MORALE & MOTIVATION

Good morale is closely linked to
motivation, which is:

- How to get people to do things
  willingly and well

- The motives to act that
  people have

This is an important subject, which has
a great impact on discipline and grievances.

MORALE & MOTIVATION

You can recognise motivation and discipline in a company by:

- Appearance of premises, eg: clean and tidy
- Appearance of people, eg: appropriate clothing
- Conduct of people, eg: the *buzz,* showing respect for others
- Workflow, eg: unhurried, appears organised

IMPROVING MOTIVATION AT WORK

Here are some suggestions to help you improve motivation within your area or department:

- Know your people
- Consider the *people aspect* in all decisions
- Think first before jumping in (this can prevent later embarrassment)
- Appreciate that differences in people can be interesting
- Accept that some people will need more direction and guidance than others
- Try to see things from other people's perspective
- Do not automatically censor ideas just because you feel uncomfortable with them

SPEND TIME ON PREVENTION

IMPROVING MOTIVATION AT WORK

- Remain flexible in attitude and approach; highly necessary in a quickly changing environment
- List as many ideas to motivate as you can
- Take time to introduce changes
- Evaluate and monitor results
- Ring the changes regularly as motivation changes
- Give praise and thanks when they are due

HOW TO
INTERVIEW

HANDLING THE DISCIPLINE INTERVIEW

No two discipline interviews will be the same. The following, therefore, aims to give best practice guidelines only.

Step 1: Preparing for the interview

- Have the facts available
- Define what the problem is, but do not prejudge
- Advise the employee of the time and date they are required to attend an interview and give details of the disciplinary procedure
- Advise the employee that they have the right to be represented

HANDLING THE DISCIPLINE INTERVIEW

Step 1: Preparing for the interview

- Arrange to have a second member of management to take notes and act as a witness (especially if the employee is to be accompanied)

- Think through how the employee might defend their position

- Note down specific things you wish to raise

- Think through and review how you will handle the interview. For example, keep the approach formal and polite and encourage the employee to talk freely. Use questions to clarify and check. Try not to get involved in arguments and do not make personal remarks. Avoid any threatening body language

- Arrange a quiet room and time when there will be no interruptions

- Remember, above all, your purpose is to inform and correct performance or bad behaviour and to prevent it from happening again

HANDLING THE DISCIPLINE INTERVIEW

Step 2:   Starting the interview

- Explain to the employee the purpose of the interview and how it will be conducted
- If they have come alone, then inform them of their right to be accompanied
- Advise on the substance of the complaint and show any evidence you have, such as witness statements
- Show any other backup information

HANDLING THE DISCIPLINE INTERVIEW

Step 3: Core of the interview

- Ask the employee if they have any explanations

- Remember, the purpose of the interview is not to catch out the employee but to discover the truth

- Establish if the employee is prepared to accept that something wrong has been done

- Give the employee time to state their case, present evidence and call witnesses

- Evaluate the response and reasons given

- Explore further, if needed

- If the explanation is accepted, stop the proceedings

- If the explanation is *thin*, adjourn to check out any disputed facts

Note: Adjournments may also be needed to allow any *cooling off* if the interview gets heated or over-emotional. Suspending the employee on pay may allow them time to calm down and return for a full investigation.

HANDLING THE DISCIPLINE INTERVIEW

Step 4: Closing the interview

- Decide what version of the facts you believe to be true
- Consider what action is needed for improvement and whether disciplinary action is needed
- Tell the employee of your decision
- Leave the employee in no doubt as to the nature of the penalty and the improvement needed
- Inform the employee of their right of appeal, giving details of the person to whom the appeal should be made and the time limit

HANDLING THE DISCIPLINE INTERVIEW

Step 4: Closing the interview

If needed, check out your company formal appeal procedure, which will cover the following:

- Time limits
- Speedy dealing with appeals
- Having the appeal heard by a higher authority
- Details of the actions that can be taken
- Opportunity for the employee to introduce new evidence

HANDLING THE DISCIPLINE INTERVIEW

Step 4: Closing the interview

- Close the interview by summarising details of the problem, the action taken and the right of appeal
- Write to the employee confirming the action taken
- Make brief notes of the interview
- Keep a record in your incidents diary
- Inform your boss of the action taken
- Check to see if your action has returned the employee to the accepted performance/behaviour

HANDLING THE GRIEVANCE INTERVIEW

The employee initiates a grievance, so the first you may hear about it is a request for a grievance interview. The problem will then be verbally presented.

If the grievance is sent in writing, acknowledge this and suggest a specific meeting time. You then have some time to investigate.

Step 1: Preparing for the interview

- Get as many facts available as you can
- See what the problem could be
- Advise the employee they have the right to be represented
- Arrange for a second member of management to take notes and act as a witness (especially if the employee is to be accompanied)

HANDLING THE GRIEVANCE INTERVIEW

Step 1: Preparing for the interview

- Think through how the employee might put their position

- Note down specific things you wish to raise

- Think through and review how you will handle the interview. For example, keep the approach formal and polite and encourage the employee to talk freely. Use questions to clarify and check. Try not to get involved in arguments and do not make personal remarks. Avoid any threatening body language

- Arrange a quiet room and time when there will be no interruptions

- Remember, above all, your purpose is to allow the employee to air their grievance, to establish the *before*/causes and to remove the dissatisfaction if at all possible

HANDLING THE GRIEVANCE INTERVIEW

Step 2: Starting the interview
- Put the employee at ease
- Encourage them to talk
- Listen sincerely and sympathetically
- Keep your temper

Step 3: Core of the interview
- Get a clear picture of the real problem being expressed
- Encourage the employee to give their solution
- Keep listening and show you are doing so by taking notes, reflecting back what has been said, nodding, maintaining eye contact and showing you are interested

HANDLING THE GRIEVANCE INTERVIEW

Step 4: Closing the interview

Two options here:

- Do not shift the blame. If you are not sure, defer a decision and proceed to Step 5.
- Say what you can or cannot do and proceed to Step 6.

Step 5: Investigating the grievance further (if necessary)

- Be thorough
- Gather all the facts you can
- Review the employee's record for any clues
- Discuss with others whose experience may help you
- Check on any previous similar problems and see what was done then
- Ask your boss and HR/personnel people if you are at all uncertain
- Review Steps 1 and 2 and, as appropriate, Steps 3 and 4

HOW TO INTERVIEW

HANDLING THE GRIEVANCE INTERVIEW

Step 6: Making a decision about the grievance

- If you or the company are wrong, then say so

- If the employee's problem is unfounded, then explain why

- If the employee presents additional facts, consider, re-check; maybe adjourn for further investigation (and back to Step 5)

- Confirm your answer in writing; say *Why* as well as *What*.
  Be courteous and give a clear statement of the significant facts

- If the employee will not accept your decision, then explain the company formal appeals procedure

HANDLING THE GRIEVANCE INTERVIEW

Step 7: Following up

- Follow through on your answer; if you have committed to specific action, then you must do this

- Check with the employee to see if the problem has been eliminated

- Follow up at regular intervals to see that the *before* triggers and causes do not recur

- Keep records of what you have done in your incidents diary

DISMISSAL

DISMISSAL

BE SURE

People who are going to be fired are rarely happy about it, so be sure, convince yourself and be satisfied that you have tried to help the employee to improve and to succeed.

Always remember that if you dismiss someone unfairly, you leave yourself open to the involvement of employment tribunals and, increasingly, legal action. Every year, in the UK, there are over 100,000 employment tribunals.

This is a large waste, which also reflects some poor management practices.

DISMISSAL

UNFAIR DISMISSAL

A dismissal will be unfair unless it is concerned with:

- Conduct (misconduct or gross misconduct).
- Capability, such as the inability to do the job, incapability due to ill health.
- Redundancy, that is a reduced requirement for an employee to do the job for which they were recruited.
- Contravening laws, such as a driver who loses a licence and is unable to perform the job.
- Other substantial reasons. The emphasis here is on *substantial*; this is not a *catch all* reason for dismissal. For example, a valid reason could be if your company were to lose a major client because the client will no longer deal with your employee.

DISMISSAL

HANDLING THE DISMISSAL

Best practice guidelines follow:

Step 1: Preparation for the dismissal interview

- Review all documents and be sure the employee has been warned of the possible outcomes of dismissal in all the previous discipline procedures or, if dealing with proven gross misconduct, review to ensure that all the correct procedures have been followed

- Get your HR/personnel people to check and to attend the interview

- Review money owed to the employee and any money owed by the employee to the company

- Review again all the details in all the stages and steps that have brought you to this point

- Arrange for the employee to attend, and ensure they know why they are required

- Ensure the employee is aware of their right to be represented at the interview

- Arrange a quiet room for the interview with no interruptions

HANDLING THE DISMISSAL

Step 2: The dismissal interview

- Explain why the meeting is taking place
- State your case
- Be firm, calm and brief
- Answer briefly any questions
- Say clearly when the employee is to leave

DISMISSAL

HANDLING THE DISMISSAL

Step 3: Closing the interview

- Reach an agreement on the final money issues
- Ask for all appropriate company property to be returned
- Agree a method for handling ongoing mail and messages
- Inform the employee of their right of appeal, giving details of the person to whom the appeal should be made and the time limit

HANDLING THE DISMISSAL

Step 4: Following up

- Have the final money ready for the day they leave
- Make sure all company property has been returned
- Reflect on any learning lessons
- Enter up your incidents diary

THE FIVE PER CENT VIEW OF DISCIPLINE & GRIEVANCE

Let's put some of this book into perspective.

Let me assume that people are evenly distributed between good and poor performers.

Employee's Performance

Very Poor	Poor	Average	Good	Very Good
5% of people	20% of people	50% of people	20% of people	5% of people

DISMISSAL

THE FIVE PER CENT VIEW OF DISCIPLINE & GRIEVANCE

 ARROW ONE

This is the manager's problem. Here 5 per cent of your people are problems. Maybe, if you are not careful, 95 per cent of your time is being spent on only 5 per cent of the people. This cannot be good or right for an efficient and effective company.

This book has, however, addressed what needs to be done in this 5 per cent problem area.

 ARROW TWO

This is the manager's task. This is, simply, to move more people from the left to the right to make them all good performers.

The positive message here is that this involves over 90 per cent of people.
Thinking and believing this is what management is about will lead you to take the appropriate actions. This book has hinted at some of the important areas to be considered to make people good performers, to stop unacceptable behaviour, prevent unauthorised absence, etc.

DISMISSAL

PREVENTING DISCIPLINE & GRIEVANCE PROBLEMS

We conclude with a view on what is needed to prevent having to deal continually with discipline and grievances.

A recipe to make *Managing People the Right Way*

- Start with good people
- Mix in clear rules and procedures
- Add the vital ingredient of communication
- Cook continually with plenty of motivation
- Finally, rejoice and reward correct performance

DISMISSAL

PREVENTING DISCIPLINE & GRIEVANCE PROBLEMS

The *recipe* will bring you good results if you ensure that you take the following actions:

- Make sure your people know the standards that are required
- Communicate clearly how they are able to achieve these standards
- Motivate them to progress in the direction required
- Reward them and continually communicate and motivate so that standards are maintained

And for a small minority – five per cent? – then, as a last resort, you will have to apply discipline procedures when the required standards are not being met.

About the Author

Stuart Emmett MSc. BA(Hon), FICT, FILT, FIFF, MCIPD
Stuart started his career in freight forwarding, followed by a move into consultancy, specialising in the analysis of freight transport costs and service factors, and the tendering/selection of freight service providers. After gaining a BA from the Open University, he took up a job in Nigeria for five years. On return to the UK, an MSc at Cranfield in Transport Studies was followed by a move into third party distribution, with a position on the board.

Stuart entered the people development business full time in 1990, getting involved with the start up of the training service to the Institute of Logistics, which resulted in a directorship with the company. Since 1998, Stuart has had his own business and has greatly enjoyed the independence the new found freedom gives him to undertake other types of work, including a return to Nigeria to train, and writing and designing material in other areas and subjects. He has also acted as a coach and mentor to individuals/groups, and as a catalyst/consultant to effect change.

He remains particularly interested in all the 'people issues' of management processes. Stuart currently trades under the name "Learn & Change" believing that in times of change, it is the learners who will be better able to successfully inherit the future.

Contact
Stuart Emmett, Learn & Change
E mail: Stuart@semmett.freeserve.co.uk Telefax: +44 (0)127 463 5342

THE MANAGEMENT POCKETBOOK SERIES

Pocketbooks

Appraisals
Assertiveness
Balance Sheet
Business Planning
Business Presenter's
Business Writing
Challengers
Coaching
Communicator's
Controlling Absenteeism
Creative Manager's
Cross-cultural Business
Cultural Gaffes
Customer Service
Decision-making
Discipline
E-commerce
E-customer Care
Empowerment
Facilitator's

Handling Complaints
Improving Efficiency
Improving Profitability
Induction
Influencing
Interviewer's
Key Account Manager's
Learner's
Managing Budgets
Managing Cashflow
Managing Change
Managing Your Appraisal
Manager's
Manager's Training
Marketing
Meetings
Mentoring
Motivation
Negotiator's
Networking

People Manager's
Performance Management
Personal Success
Project Management
Problem Behaviour
Quality
Sales Excellence
Salesperson's
Self-managed Development
Starting In Management
Stress
Teamworking
Telephone Skills
Telesales
Thinker's
Time Management
Trainer Standards
Trainer's

Pocketsquares

Leadership: Sharing The Passion
The Great Presentation Scandal
The Great Training Robbery
Hook Your Audience

Pocketfiles

Trainer's Blue Pocketfile of
Ready-to-use Exercises

Trainer's Green Pocketfile of
Ready-to-use Exercises

Trainer's Red Pocketfile of
Ready-to-use Exercises

Audio Cassettes

Tips for Presenters
Tips for Trainers

ORDER FORM

Your details

Name _____

Position _____

Company _____

Address _____

_____

_____

Telephone _____

Fax _____

E-mail _____

VAT No. (EC companies) _____

Your Order Ref _____

Please send me:

	No. copies

The Discipline _____ Pocketbook ☐

The _____ Pocketbook ☐

The _____ Pocketbook ☐

The _____ Pocketbook ☐

The _____ Pocketbook ☐

Order by Post

MANAGEMENT POCKETBOOKS LTD
14 EAST STREET ALRESFORD HAMPSHIRE SO24 9EE UK

Order by Phone, Fax or Internet
Telephone: +44 (0)1962 735573
Facsimile: +44 (0)1962 733637
E-mail: sales@pocketbook.co.uk
Web: www.pocketbook.co.uk

Customers in USA should contact:
Stylus Publishing, LLC, 22883 Quicksilver Drive,
Sterling, VA 20166-2012
Telephone: 703 661 1581 or 800 232 0223
Facsimile: 703 661 1501 E-mail: styluspub@aol.com